Handwriting
Practice

My name is

_____

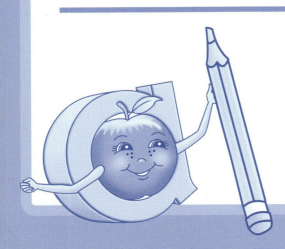

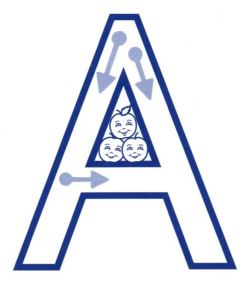

A nnie A pple

A A A A

Aa Aa Aa

How many ants?

Search for ants on these two pages, then
trace over the correct number.

123

Bouncy Ben

B B B B

Bb Bb Bb

How many balls?

Search for balls on these two pages, then
trace over the correct number.

1 2 3 4

Clever Cat

How many cakes?

Trace over the correct number.

123

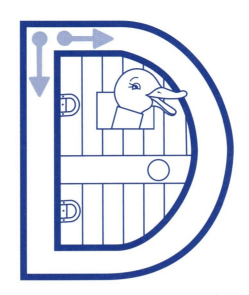

Dippy Duck

D D D D

Dd Dd Dd

How many dogs?

1234

Trace over the correct number.

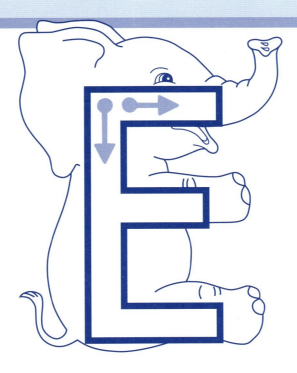

Eddy Elephant

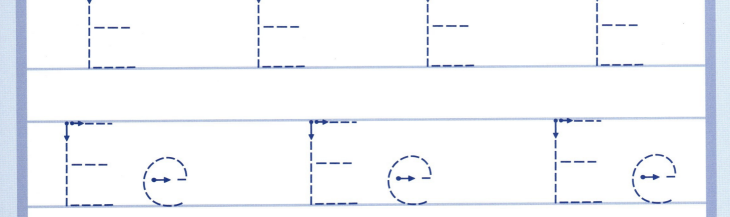

How many eggs?

1 2 3 4 5

Trace over the correct number.

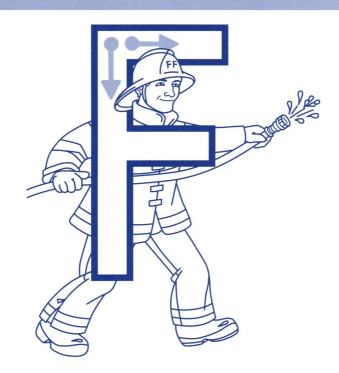

Firefighter Fred

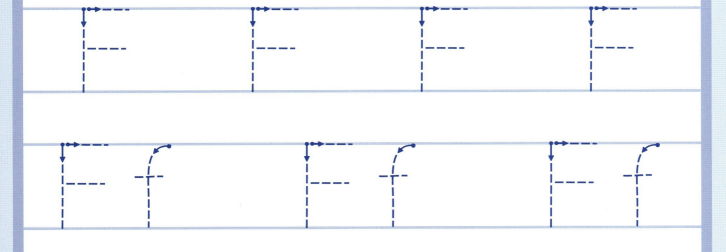

How many fish?

Trace over the correct number.

1 2 3 4 5

Golden **G**irl

G G G G

Gg Gg Gg

How many gloves?

Trace over the correct number.

1 2 3 4 5

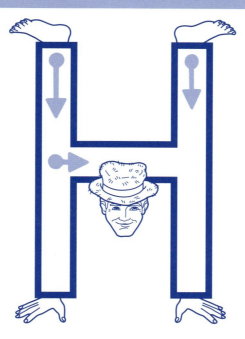

Harry Hat Man

How many hats?

Trace over the correct number.

1 2 3 4 5

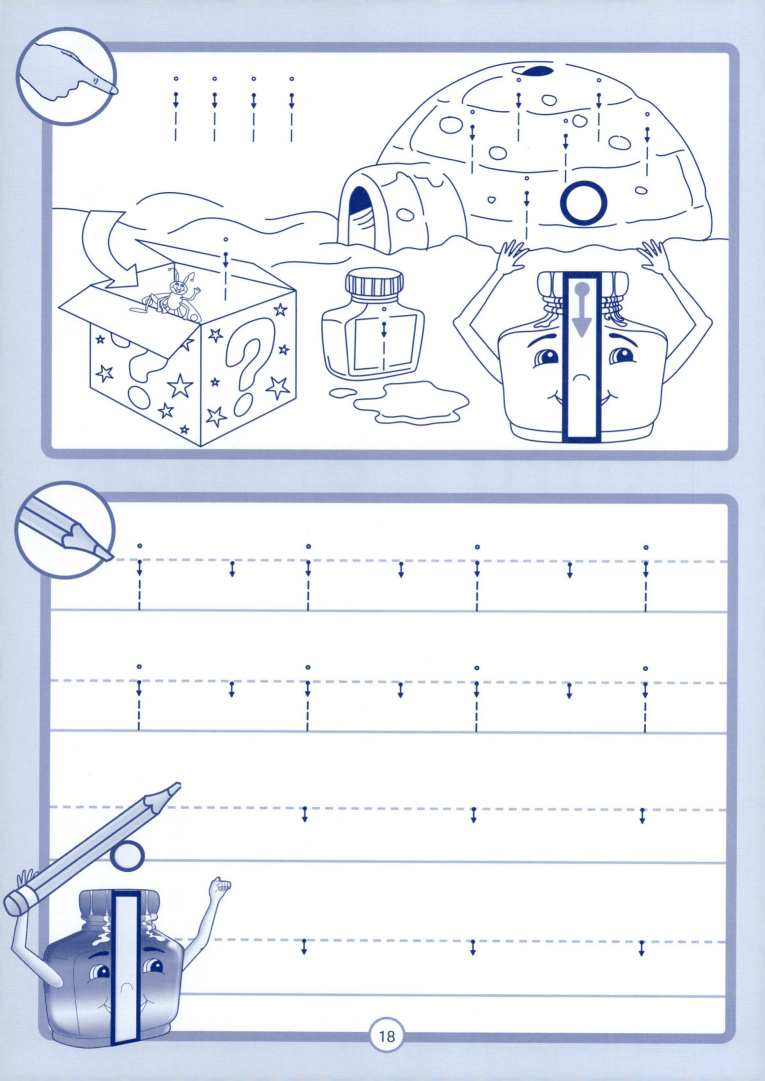

I mpy Ink

How many insects?

Trace over the correct number.

1 2 3 4 5 6

Jumping Jim

How many jars?

Trace over the correct number.

1 2 3 4 5 6

Kicking King

K K K K

Kk Kk Kk Kk

How many kites?

1 2 3 4 5 6

Trace over the correct number.

Lucy Lamp Light

How many lemons?

Trace over the correct number.

1 2 3 4 5 6

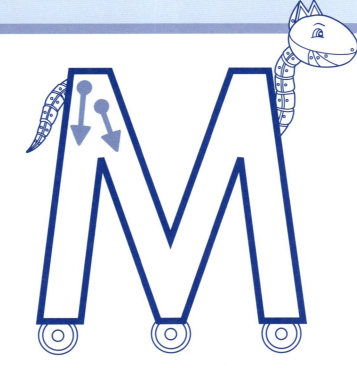

Munching Mike

M M M M M

Mm Mm Mm

How many mice?

1 2 3 4 5 6

Trace over the correct number.

Noisy Nick

N N N N

Nn Nn Nn

Count and trace over all the numbers.

1 2 3 4 5 6 7 8 9

Oscar Orange

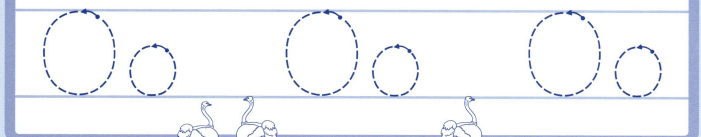

How many ostriches?

Trace over the correct number.

2 4 6 8

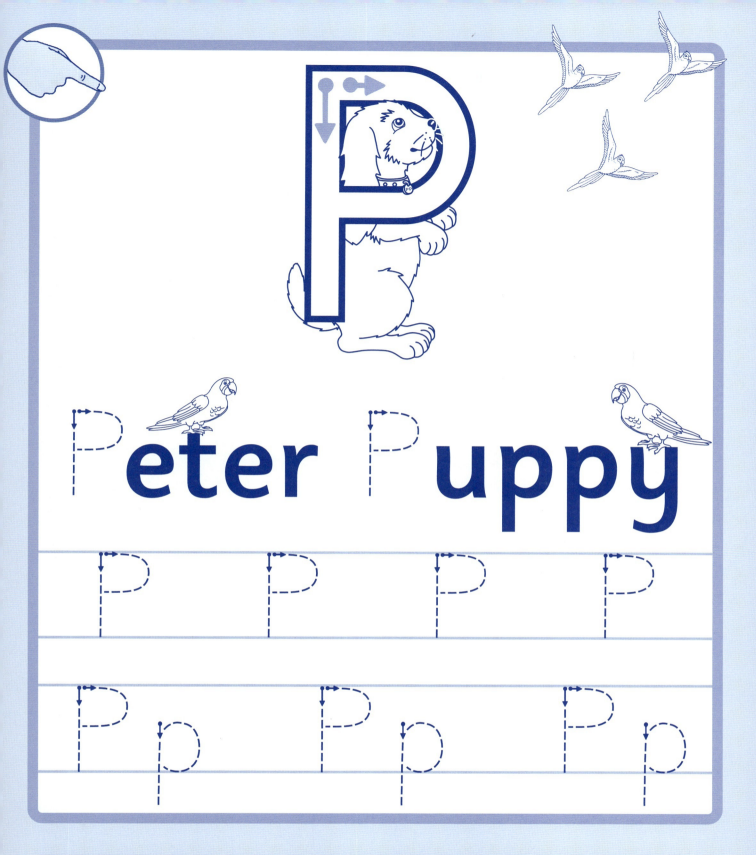

Peter Puppy

P P P P

Pp Pp Pp

How many parrots?
Trace over the correct number.

1 3 5 7

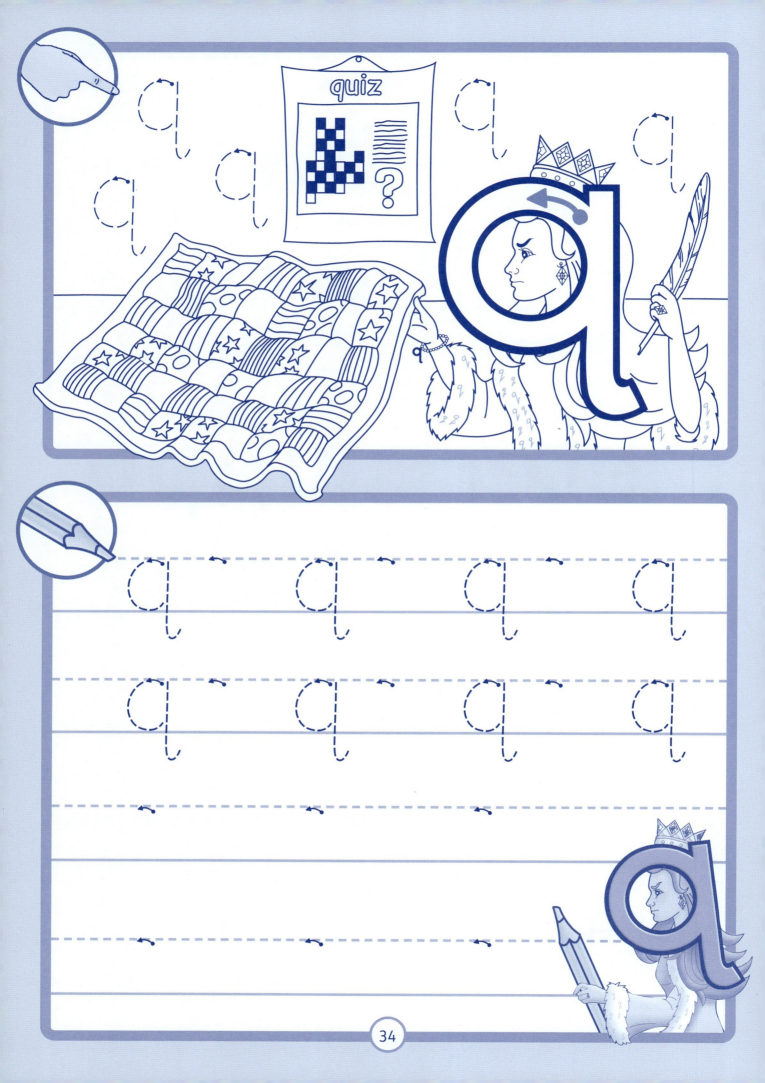

quiz

q

Quarrelsome Queen

How many quills?

Trace over the correct number.

2 4 6 8

rockets

Red Robot

R R R R

Rr Rr Rr

How many rings?

Trace over the correct number.

1 3 5 7 9

Sammy Snake

S S S S

S s S s S s S s

How many stars?

6789

Trace over the correct number.

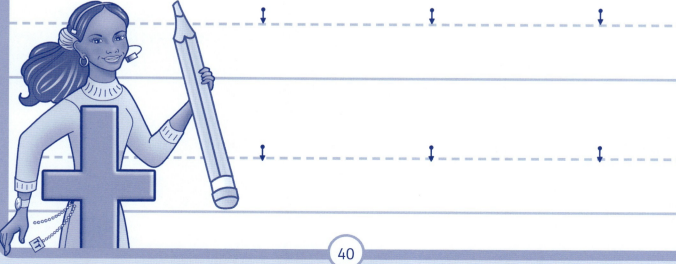

Talking Tess

T T T T

t t t t

How many teddies?

Trace over the correct number.

6789

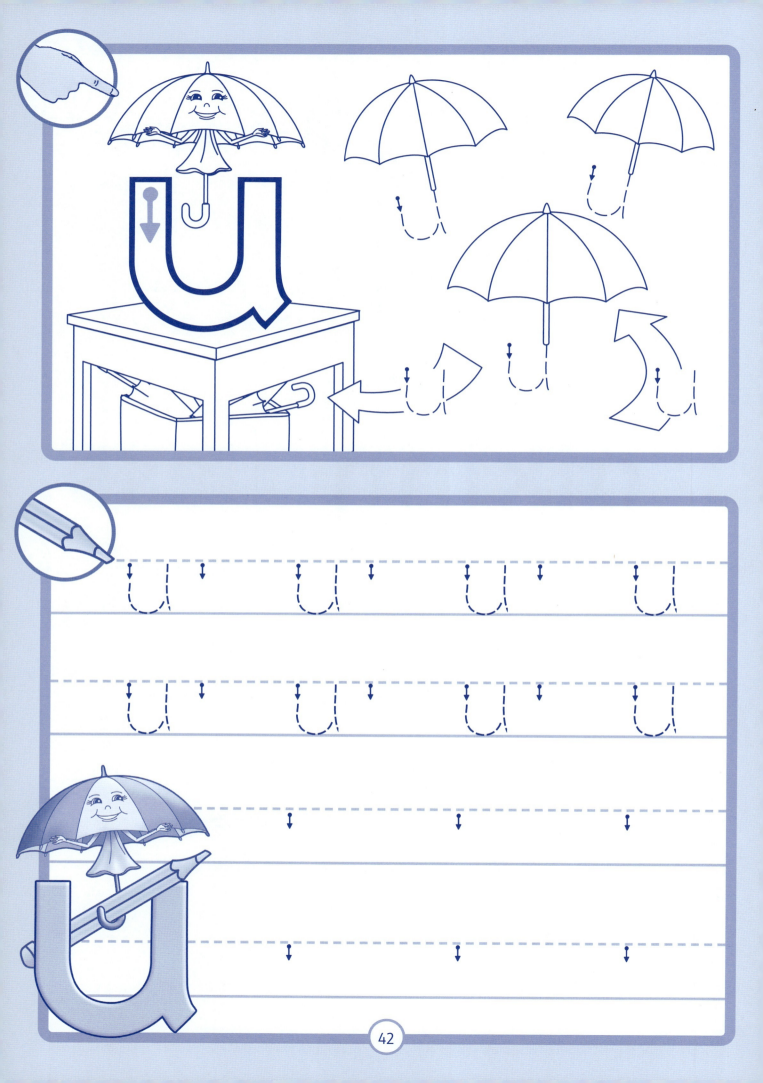

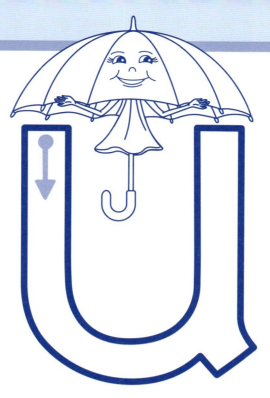

Uppy **U**mbrella

How many umbrellas?

Trace over the correct number.

6 7 8 9

43

Vicky Violet

Count and trace over all the numbers.

1 2 3 4 5 6 7 8 9

Walter Walrus

W W W W W

Ww Ww Ww Ww

Count and trace over all the numbers.

1 2 3 4 5 6 7 8 9

Fix-it Max

Count and trace over all the numbers.

1 2 3 4 5 6 7 8 9

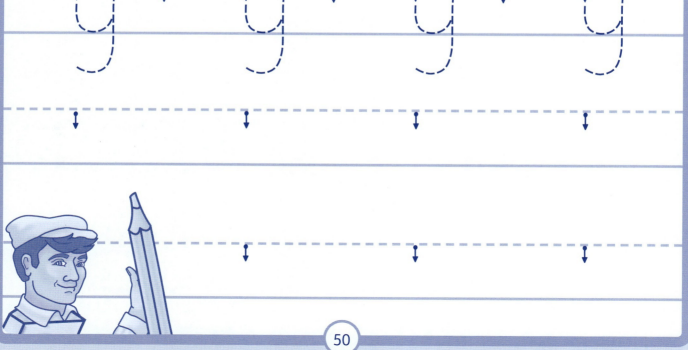

Yo-yo Man

Count and trace over all the numbers.

123456789

Zig Zag Zebra

Write all the numbers from 1-9.

Handwriting Songs

Annie Apple

At the leaf begin.
Go round the apple this way.
Then add a line down
so Annie won't roll away.

Bouncy Ben

Brush down Ben's big, long ears.
Go up and round his head
so his face appears!

Clever Cat

Curve round Clever Cat's
face to begin.
Then gently tickle her
under her chin.

Dippy Duck

Draw Dippy Duck's back.
Go round her tum.
Go up to her head.
Then down you come!

Eddy Elephant

Ed has a headband.
Draw it and then
stroke round his head
and his trunk to the end.

Firefighter Fred

First draw Fred's helmet.
Then go down a way.
Give him some arms
and he'll put out the blaze.

Golden Girl

Go round Golden Girl's head.
Go down her golden hair.
Then curve to make her swing,
so she can sit there.

Harry Hat Man

Hurry from the Hat Man's head down
to his heel on the ground.
Go up and bend his knee over,
so he'll hop while he makes hisÀ-
sound.

Impy Ink

Inside the ink bottle
draw a line.
Add an inky dot. That's fine!

Jumping Jim

Just draw down Jim,
bending his knees.
Then add the one ball
which everyone sees.

Kicking King

Kicking King's body
is a straight stick.
Add his arm, then his leg,
so he can kick!

Lucy Lamp Light

Lucy looks like one long line.
Go straight from head to foot
and she's ready to shine!

Munching Mike

Make Munching Mike's
back legÀfirst,
then his second leg, and third,
so he can go munch-munching in a
word.

Noisy Nick

'Now bang my nail,'
NoisyÀNick said.
'Go up and over aroundÀmyÀhead.'

Oscar Orange

On Oscar Orange startÀatÀtheÀtop.
Go all the way round him,
and... then stop.

Peter Puppy

Pat Peter Puppy properly.
First stroke down his ear,
then up and round his face
so he won't shed a tear.

Quarrelsome Queen

Quickly go round the
Queen'sÀcross face.
Then comb her beautiful hairÀinto
place.

Red Robot

Run down Red Robot's body.
Go up to his arm andÀhisÀhand.
Then watch out for this robot
roaming round Letterland.

Sammy Snake

Start at Sam's head
where he can see.
Stroke down to his tail,
oh so care-ful-ly!

Talking Tess

Tall as a tower make
TalkingÀTess stand.
Go from head to toe,
and then from hand to hand.

Uppy Umbrella

Under the umbrella
draw a shape like a cup.

Then draw a straight line
so it won't tip up.

Vicky Violet

Very neatly, start at the top.
Draw down your vase, thenÀupÀand
stop.

Walter Walrus

When you draw the WalrusÀwells,
with wild and wavy water,
whizz down and up andÀthen...,
whizz down and up again.

Fix-it Max

Fix two sticks, to look likeÀthis.
That's how to draw a littleÀkiss.

Yo-yo Man

You first make the yo-yo sack
on the Yo-yo Man's back,
and then go down to his toes
so he can sell his yo-yos.

Zig Zag Zebra

Zip along Zig Zag's nose.
Stroke her neck...,
stroke her back...
Zzzoom! Away she goes.

Letterland Characters

Annie Apple   Bouncy Ben   Clever Cat   Dippy Duck   Eddy Elephant   Firefighter Fred   Golden Girl

Harry Hat Man   Impy Ink   Jumping Jim   Kicking King   Lucy Lamp Light   Munching Mike

Noisy Nick   Oscar Orange   Peter Puppy   Quarrelsome Queen   Red Robot   Sammy Snake

Talking Tess   Uppy Umbrella   Vicky Violet   Walter Walrus   Fix-it Max   Yellow Yo-yo Man   Zig Zag Zebra